A Peasant's Poems

Dennis Woodfine

Drawings by Pamela Thornton

To order additional copies of this book, contact:
Xlibris
0800-056-3182
www.xlibrispublishing.co.uk
Orders@ Xlibrispublishing.co.uk

I dedicate this book to the beautiful
memories of Frederic and Lily Woodfine.

Veronica's Ordination

Marbury Church 28/11/2017

This hallowed place was full

No one came out into the highways

The byways and the hedges to compel us to come in

We came for the atonement of our sin

We came from our various ways

for the joy of singing a hymn

To give praise

But most of all to see our Veronica sworn in!

Oh, the pageantry the tradition the majesty

of that ceremony

there was no "Lutine Bell" to ring

No cacophony of trumpets there

but in that sanctuary

LISTEN! My friend, LISTEN! Please

Shsssss Shssssssssss!

LISTEN! LISTEN! With me to the angels sing

Pictured is one of Veronica's churches — Whitewell

The Carden Arms

It was at our good old pub The Carden Arms.

Where the locals gathered from the cottages and farms,

There was Jack Davies from the mill,

Sid Jones had brought his Uncle Bill,

There was Uncle Ron and Auntie Phil,

Alf Jones and Mabel,

and the Irish lads from the Cholmondely Stable,

There were two lovely lasses who worked at the vets,

The landlord was taking a couple of illegal bets,

The evening sun was casting shadows on the wall,

A good time was being had by all,

Jack Harris was drinking with Pete Mcann,

When his wife put her head around the door,

Come Jack Please,

Come as quick as you can,

There is a heifer trying to calve,

Jack grabbed his hat and his scarf,

And did as his better half had bid,

Then Bob Worth,

Put in his half pennyworth,

"I would not have that" he said!

"I would stop that, just like that" as he snapped his fingers in the air

What a fallacy! What a farce! What a snub!

She just wanted him out of the pub!

Is he a man or a mouse!?

Strikes me he is not the master in his own house

What a fallacy! What a farce!

He just went without any argument,

He is under a petticoat government,

Heifer having a calf!

I do not believe that tale!

Not by one half!

What a fallacy, what a farce!

Then to the delight of that company

In came Bob's wife Queenie

She was about 5 feet two

And weighed about eight stones, wet through

She waived a finger under his nose as only a feisty woman can do

"Do you think that I AM GOING TO WORK ALL HOURS at Stretton Hall?

Just for you to come in here and PEE MY HOUSE KEEPING MONEY UP A WALL?"

"Come on out of it YOU DRUNKEN GIT!"

For a moment, there was silence and a bit of a stand off

Someone gave a nervous cough

Then Bob turned quietly towards the door

Some wag whispered "what a fallacy! What a farce!"

Then there was an uproar

When Queenie shouted "COME ON!"

And kicked him up the arse.

Lost Souls

Dead! Gone! Long ago,
The you that was you
and the me, that was me
Of a decade or so ago,
Lost amongst the woods,
Neath Larkton hill,

Last night, alone, I revisited,
A one time, long ago,
Much favoured rendezvous
The moon and stars were silver,
The sky was blue
There was a rustle from the leaves

The unmistakeable scent,
Of your hair,
Whispering, laughter.
The sound of footsteps there,
And yet, strangely?!
No footprints in the Snow

The Nightmare

I am walking OK now with my plastic hip and my plastic knee,
I walked out from my flat across the plastic grass,
and sat on the plastic seat and looked across the garden to see a dead bird under a dead tree
and slowly became drowsy and sleep came to me

The radio came to life EMERGENCY, EMERGENCY the is the U.K. SPACE CONTROLE
We are under attack
THIS IS NOT A HOAX, REPEAT THIS IS NOT A HOAX,
Several missiles have been launched against the U.K. AND THE U.S.A.
A defensive shield has been deployed
Massive retaliation is in progress
Go in doors IMMEDIATLY
Draw curtains and blinds
where possible stack furniture against the windows
Fill all available utensils with drinking water;
do NOT go outside under any circumstances
Do not look out through the windows!
REPEAT this is an emergency
REPEAT THIS IS AN EMERGENCY

This is it then Armageddon
Most forms of communication had been hacked destroyed got at,
I thought of my brother, we had not spoken for ten years
some daft quarrel over a few thousand pounds,
or some thing or other
I tried to ring him but the phone was dead
no chance now to make peace!
Or to recall those bitter words which were said!

FOUR PM

It was already dark,

the sky was a dull red glow with all the radioactive dust in the stratosphere

The radio came back to life

U.K. space station reporting

there "is a lake where London used to be!" most of the world's cities

Are DUST IN THE SEA.

The trees in the amazon are all DYING

As I stirred from my slumber I could hear a baby crying

DAD! DAD Cup of tea?

Not now love! I REALLY need to speak to my brother!

Sweet Memories

I remember so well the 21st birthday party,

That my family did for me

Back in 1963

Dear Uncle Bill broke wind fantastically

What it lacked in melody

It made up for in velocity

And potency

A couple of flies dropped off the wall,

The cat bolted into the hall,

Auntie Ethel's face was like a huge crimson rose,

The dog put both his paws over his nose,

Mum was not best pleased at such vulgarity

and she swore that it made

The cream in her trifle curdle

Big Aunt Vic was apoplectic

She waived her arms about and shouted Oh dear! Oh dear!

I feel sick!

Then she turned purple

and went out to slacken her girdle

Oh yes, the memories sweet memories!

Negotiation

A Countrywoman to a handsome council foreman.

Can I have some of that tarmac for me drive?

I know that there is talk of austerity

but I think that with a bit of jiggery-pokery

you could wangle a few tonnes for me

I will give you a tenner and brew yer some tea.

What's yer name? OH, oh Jack,

OH and yer think the superintendent

Would give yer the sack

Well don't you worry about that old so and so!

He is married to me cousin Floe,

It would be in the family,

If you did me drive for me

You want a bit more, what will it take?

Tell yer what, I will bake you a cake

and up the money to thirty!

Shaking your head, Goodness me!

I will chuck in two dozen eggs newly laid,

Surely at that you would be well paid!

No, no, well I am not going down on my knees

but I will chuck in 5lbs of newly picked peas.

That's got to be a good deal!

STILL NO! HOW FAR HAVE I GOT TO GO!?

Tell you what I will cook yer a meal

and give you two jars of honey straight from me hive

If somehow or other you can do me drive

STILL NO! IM GETTING EXASPERATED

and frustrated!

Tell you what Jack

Forget everything I have said,

Forget the tarmac

and just come with me to BED!

Young Love

I will tell you a tale about a Dalmatian
Victor Algernon Marmaduke,
A dog of ill repute
He belonged to Jack and Rosie Swain,
At Home Farm, by the institute,
Down Church Lane,
He had a pedigree (they said)
As long as your arm,
but you could have fooled me!
I reckon that as well as the official mating
his mother had
done some unofficial,
Sly, round the corner dating,
and looking at Vick she had not been that choosy
and was probably a bit of a floosy

When I tell you what he did to me
Back in the spring time of 1973
You will (I am sure) forgive me
For casting aspersions
At his pedigree
It was at the old school at Manley,
That I met Jennie Lee,
She was fifteen, same as me!
Only she was going on 23

She was voted sports personality of the year,
and she looked so pretty, so seductive!
In her hockey gear
My heart used to flutter
When she was near
I asked her out (once or twice)
She was always very nice
when she declined
Not coming she said, if you don't mind?

Ask one of the other girls
Then she laughed and threw back her curls.
Which did nothing at all the cool my fevered brow!
I had to do something to win her favours,
Somehow!

Then something happened that upped, my status by a few degrees,
I had a new bike, a brand new Hercules
IT was bought with 3 years of saved paper round fees!
As I thought I was on a winning streak
Once more to Jennie I would speak,
A faint heart they said, never won a fair lady
and If I asked her, well maybe, maybe!
to my great delight she agreed
that we should meet by the park,
on Sunday at half past two
As I cycled down Church Lane, towards our rendezvous,
Life seemed almost too good to be true
The church bells were ringing
And my heart was singing
I was riding quite fast
I did not want to be late!

Then I spotted Victor Algernon Marmaduke.
By his farm gate, where he squatted
That Vic, that horrible mutt, licked his lips
and sniggered and plotted
He anticipated and he waited,
Then he came out like a rocket
I never saw the like!
He grabbed me coat pocket
and pulled me off me bike
I lay semi-conscious on the ground
I felt a bit sick and queer.
Then to add insult to injury he came over and peed in me ear
and me new bike with the latest 9 speed gears
Was bent over about 30 degrees
I had intended to get there by any means
and now me bum was hanging out of me jeans!

Mrs Swain was a big lady

With a fist like a steam hammer

Which she waved at me over the wall

Her voice was something between a shout and a wail

You have mutilated my POOR "Vic"

You have run over his tail,

Yer nothing but A LUNATIC

Yer WANT PUTTING IN JAIL

And if it was down to me

I would throw AWAY THE KEY

I was (of course) unable to keep our meeting

When next I met Jennie I did not get much of a greeting

I tried to explain

She said I knew it!

You had your chance

GET lost!

You blew it!

Embarrasing Modern Technology

Cattle feed rep and Mrs. Jones in the farm kitchen 1952

My word Mrs. Jones that is a smart television!

Aye we got it off Fred Furnival

In time for the owd Kings funeral

We could have had a bush or a Ferguson

but we got a Ferranti

and it has given a lot of pleasure to Harry and me and all the family

but it took a lot of work and a lot of saving

and we also sold a couple of heifers and a stirk.

But as parson said, when he called last Tuesday

"You have got to embarrass modern technology"

"Mrs Jones, what's that goose doing under the telly?"

Oh that's our Floe errs sitting a dozen eggs

Err built that nest three weeks ago out of a Farms Weekly a News of the World

and a Beano.

It's the valves you see it helps to keep 'em waarm

Errs hissing a bit, but if you stop this side of the table.

Err wunner do yer any harm,

Mrs Jones now about this outstanding feed bill

£85.00 is a scary amount!

My father has instructed me that if you can't pay in full today!

I am to close your account!

Now look hear, we wunner let yer down,

but as it happens Harrys got the cheque book

and he has gone to town.

ROSIE! ROSIE! Come here and take young Mr. Pritchard

for a walk down the orchard

its cosy on that seat under the lilac tree

you can swap some jokes and get a bit friendly!

I will make him some tea.

But, dunner get squealing and aahing and oohing!

Or folk going past will wonder what you are doing

When they returned they both looked quite pink,
and mother and daughter swapped a crafty wink
There then you tell your old feller, we have been short delivered
next month when we have sold the corn everything will be covered

As Pritchard closed the farm gate the cockerel on the midden crowed
"Nice young feller that" "I hope we can pay him everything that he is owed!"
Rosie I think you have earned a rest"
Floe shuffled about as she turned her eggs in her nest
and Mrs Jones folded her arms across her ample chest
Aye she said, these days
"YOU have got to embarrass modern technology"

Charlie (My Blackbird)

What's the matter with you Charlie?

With lowered wings and feisty chest, abusing me!

From the safety of that mulberry tree,

OH! I see, you presume to object and make such a to do,

Because you fear that, I will pick all the raspberries,

and leave none for you,

Well look here Charlie, this really won't do!

I greatly value the symbiotic association we share,

I provide some feed for thee,

You sing beautiful melodies for me

But in this valley over which I have dominion,

What really counts is MY opinion,

Whilst there is many an over ripe pear,

That with you I gladly share,

In this association, the raspberries are not up for negotiation!

CHARLIE THEM'S MY RASPBERRIES

This poem is dedicated to Teresa Carberry

(district governor Lions clubs International 105bs, 2017 -2018)

Flossy

To my dog Flossie

Where did you purloin that lovely piece of sirloin?
It could not have come from far!
Perhaps around the square
or a little bit farther on?
Quite hot it was, a real treat!
Put out I expect, to cool and carve and eat
what a shock it must have been
For them to find THERE IT WAS GONE!

Did you have to lie in wait?
For this treasure to liberate!?
Or did you create a distraction?
Then execute an S.A.S. type action?
Did have to avoid a thrown boot
Curses? Threats to shoot?
When you were only trying to address
An inequality, a social unfairness!
Did it belong to Pam and Neil?
Perhaps, all secret like
I should invite them round for a meal
They could chew, at least on the bone
Of a joint that once was all their own

But putting jest aside
We did not have much to eat
when with wagging tail!
You dropped this gift at my feet
I laughed and then I Cried

Under one sky

SOMME 1916

For a moment the shriek of the shells had eased

through the smoke, which was blowing away to the east,

I saw this figure in grey with bayonet fixed running towards me

out of ammunition I expect, but I had plenty in my 303!

I pulled sight on his head

In a couple of seconds, he should have been dead.

Those seconds stretch into an eternity

little choice I had, to be killed or to kill!

In those seconds, I saw his face and he reminded me of my brother Phil

I did not pull the trigger and then in that burnt wasted, horrible land,

Fate God, call it what you will, took a hand

I heard the whistle of the shell

but could not say which way it came from in that place borrowed from hell

The blast covered us both with debris,

When I awoke, I could not find my enemy

My left leg was smashed and pouring blood

I cursed and screamed and made my way as best I could

To a dug out shrouded in smoke, in that inferno

I was losing not just blood but life, reality, sanity

I stumbled and fell outside the sanctuary, which was the dugout

and I looked once again into the face borrowed from my brother!

How long ago, I just did not know the same day nor another?

He pulled me inside, took away my gun, but in those blue eyes I saw compassion

He took off his shirt and tied it around my leg and stopped the blood,

Gave me water to drink, made me as comfortable as he could

Gunther he said, as he tapped his chest

How do! I said thank you for what you did for me I'm Stan

Nixferstan he said, well dankeschon, then bitteschon he replied

We smoked our cigarettes, side by side

He pulled out a well-thumbed photo

Frieda and Cliner Otto he said with pride

On the back was written Berlin 1915 Unter Den Linden
the stretcher-bearers came, it was time to part!
Our paths never crossed again.
But that night I prayed, that he would make it back to Unter Den Linden.
And Frieda and little Otto

Touche

Hello E.V. Hello Sally!
Long time, 5years since college,
Long time, no see,
When my name is Olive?
Why did you all call me Evie,
NO, no! SILLY!
Not Evie, E.V!

You were always a bit heavy
and you never had a boyfriend!
Some wag wrote on a wall
Olive, olive oil. EXTRA VIRGIN,
That is why we all called you E.V.

Well that was a bit catty!
Did any of those lads,
You entertained behind the bike shed,
Invite you into a warm MARITAL BED!?
Did any of them risk conception
with your scrawny bones!
Well, at the moment no.

Well I am not Evie! Or E.V.
I am MRS Jones
and before you go.
let me tell you.
She who waits WINS!
Come outside let me introduce you.
To me lovely husband and me TWINS

Flashbacks

The first hymn at the funeral was rock of ages cleft for me,

It was late in the day when we saw the crag, unconquered it seemed!

But quietly beckoned like the haven we dreamed,

about!

The service progressed, THE LORD IS MY SHEPHERD the parson said,

As we climbed the crag higher and higher,

The sheep became smaller and smaller white balls of wool,

Laid out on the patchwork quilt of fields,

Sprinkled with "dolls houses"

Across the Wirral we could see the bend in the Mersey,

By now they were singing OH LOVE THAT WILT NOT LET ME GO

But you were saying "hold me, don't let me go"

I have got cramp in my leg "hold me please hold me".

I whispered "if you go I SHALL COME TO!

But we overcame and lay down on the plateau,

and watched the setting sun

I must go back soon to that hallowed place,

and whisper your name to the wind and the sun to see if I can find you there,

That's beautiful "you said really beautiful." Thank you!

"Merci la belle ma sherrie" I replied.

You laughed out, loud and long at me.

But that did not trouble the lark singing overhead,

EARTH TO EARTH, ASHES TO ASHES, DUST TO DUST

But the soil was sticky and would not leave my hand,

"I am sorry I can't help you fasten your blouse

my hands are too mucky"

A voice, which seemed far, far away

was saying "DAD", "DAD", "COME ON DAD!"

"It's time to go!"

This poem is dedicated to Dennis' daughter, Chris.

The Pie

According to THE BARD, life is but seven ages,

and to others it's like a book with many pages,

Some other clever fellow said, life is a series of long winding streets,

and death a market place, where every man meets.

But to me a better analogy

IS that life is a big beautiful PIE,

The sort that only your mum could make,

In those dear long gone days of old.

INFANCY

Oh! The wonderment, the questions the questions of infancy,

The dawning of all the years,

If granddad went to heaven, why did mum shed so many tears?

How did Father Christmas get that wheelbarrow (Uncle Tom made for me) down the chimney?

The Christmas puddings to stir, everyone had a turn!

The glory of the huge red-berried holly burn,

from the ceiling hung with presents there on, a pocket knife for me,

a whistle for brother Ron,

A doll for little Pat

A scarf for mum for Dad, a hat.

How did the moon with all the world to light,

Find time to walk with us, to shine so bright

Down the lane under the velvet star filled night

To fetch the water from the spring

From the bubbling chortling spring,

Whose little stars sing back to their sisters in the sky?

Those lovely infant days soon went and like midnight little thief.

On the pantry bent,

That banker time

Unnoticed took back a little of what she had lent,

A bit of my pie had gone.

THE SCHOOLBOY

During those long summer holidays, which it seemed, would never end,

JESSIE MAY became my girlfriend,

"Do you realise" she said I am nearly eight?!

"You must face your responsibility AND MARRY ME"

"The ceremony can be this week,

up the hill on the bridge,

by the mill at Dawson's Creek"

With little input from me a deal was made,

And PAT was our bridesmaid,

"Oh and bring lemonade and some ham butties too!"

The girls wore sashes of blue

Had garlands of wild honeysuckle and primroses in their hair,

Carried some Campion and a rose or two

Do you promise me she said, "to love and cherish me

and to endow me with everything you have got"?

"Well yes, I suppose so, if you like!

But not me Meccano Set and not me bike!"

TEEN AGE YEARS

My sister, loved cherished, sometimes kissed,

Turned me into a juvenile misogynist,

We were chatting, as you do, about this and that,

and I happened to mention that she was getting a bit fat!

She grabbed my nose, screwed it round as far as it would go!

No wonder my mates all called me Pinocchio.

THE YOUNG MAN

Walking along the river to greet the coming dawn

A late night had become an early morn,

and there the smell of the meadow sweet mingled with hawthorn

The sun was rising to herald a new day

A warm bed was calling me home.

But a warmer lovers arms was saying stay

and there as the moon gave way to the sun on the river

and night and day and love and lust became confused.

The morning chorus was just for us,

but mum was not amused!

Many years have passed since then
Many battles fought, some lost, more of them won
I have had my share of grief
But a lot more of my share of fun,
Most of my pie has now gone
I looking at a gate in the wall,
Soon I will be moving on
But that is O.K.
Because all in all it has not been a bad PIE NOT A BAD PIE AT ALL!

Toby

DECEMBER 8TH 2002 3 AM
It was cold inside the churchyard wall
I should not have been there
I should not have been there at all!
But I had made a promise (before she died)
to dear aunt Prue
and now it was down to me.
I had a job to do!

I knew it was against the rules
That is why, earlier in the day I had hidden the tools.
Under the big laurel tree,
A white shape startled me!
As it burst from the clock tower!
It was a barn owl
As she flew lower and lower
I watched her majestic flight,
Like some spectral Lancaster on the prowl

Below the roofs under the star filled night
I heard a dog howl
and then there was the music?
A soft sweet melody
like a hymn or a lullaby.
I never found out where it came from or why?

Now I had some serious digging to do,
It would be an hour or so before I was through!
Six weeks ago, after she died,
Her little dog whimpered and cried!
I took him to see her,
So that he would understand.
A chance for him to be reconciled
That she was not coming back,
As he licked her lifeless hand, I thought it would be o.k.
That he would know why she had gone away!

But he would not eat!
We tempted him
with every kind of doggie treat, took him to the vets
Aye spent a fortune, as you do!
In the hope that we could pull him through,

We took him to the seashore,
where she used to take him to play,
the air was filled with laughter as he fetched the ball from near or far.
But now he would not even get out of the car
It was all in vain and we lost him too!

I made him a little coffin, a proper job! Elm wood and yew,
I rooted him out from under the big laurel tree
and placed him, where she wanted him to be,
I had finished before the sun rose in the east,

It would be perhaps a generation or two
before they discovered the brass plate
TOBY AND PRUE, REUNITED DECEMBER 8TH 2002

Obscene Futility

For most of those lads, some barely 17,
It was the farthest from home they had ever been,
Never set foot before in a foreign land,
But now they had been trained on Southport sand
To fight and kill,
and now they were on their way to sort out Kaiser Bill,
travelling across France to a town called Forges Les Aux,
With just five kilometres to go
For some reason unspecified,
The huge steam engine spluttered and died.
They were in open countryside,
There was no platform there,
but some jumped down to enjoy the balmy warm autumn air
there was just a few score
perhaps a hundred, no more
but then with no thought for whose they were
or why they were there
they stripped all the apple trees bare

The fruit was so juicy so sweet after all the bully beef and horse meat,
there was just one apple left on the top of the tallest tree.
One lad called Danny Pugh
decided that he was having that one too
he climbed up like MAD CAREW
By now the engineers had fixed the train
and it was on it's way again.
They all made it back with the exception of Danny Pugh,
as it clattered and puffed and hissed
Danny jumped for it and missed
His mates could only look back
at his mangled bloody body on the track

MADAM MARIE (Because of the war, a widow at 31)

with deux garcons and all her apples gone!

Had nothing to sell, no revenue!

To pay the rent which was due!

She lay abed and listened to the thunder

the mighty roar of the guns

The man made HELL,

Where girls lost their sweethearts,

and mothers their sons

and whispered "Oh lord I have nothing to sell.

For the hundredth time AMY PUGH looked out across the sea,

to where she thought her Danny would be.

It is a mistake, Oh lord let it be, that my Son,

my Danny can come back to me!

I want to see him just once more!

then she was filled with joy as he walked up from the shore,

he waved and then the VISION shimmered, faded and died.

Poor Amy wept and cried

but she felt comfort by and by that he had returned to say goodbye!

Marie knelt in her little church and prayed for absolution

that she would not go to hell!

Because in desperation she had sold the only thing, she had left to sell.

Her granddaughter does not know

that the flowers that grow

a glory of red and yellow

along the old railway track are from the seeds shed

from the flowers that Marie placed a century ago

to mark the place where Danny Pugh bled and died.

They were from the first cash she "earned "from the soldiers at

Forges les aux.

The Pugh family do not know what to make of the illuminated address
the mayor sent all those years ago
Your son it said
DIED FOR KING AND COUNTRY
HE DIED A HERO
HE DIED FOR YOU AND ME

Did Danny die for you and me?
Or did he die because like mother Eve
he could not resist an apple on a tree
OH NO! He died because of war,
THAT SCROUGE OF HUMANITY!
THAT BLASPHEMY!
THAT OBSCENE FUTILITITY!

A lady looking at a picture of a soldier.

Ode To A New Lion

If you can keep your wind,

When all around are losing theirs,

and blaming it on you,

yet make allowance for other members too.

If you can refrain from

throwing yourself off the church tower in despair

If you feel the support, you seek,

Just is not there!

If you can stand two hours

Of seemingly endless and fruitless debate

Then take a rollicking from your partner

For going home late.

But stick with us,

You will find, we have a lot of fun,

If you find you can help us make

Just one! Sick kid smile

Then it will have all been worthwhile

A new world will be yours

and that which is more,

YOU WILL BE A LION, MY SON!

No Regrets

An old timer lay down on a seat by the cross,
In the little town called Malpas.
As he slept, he dreamed,
He was a lad again,
With Maddocks, Corbet, Bradley Harding and Bell,
Sliding on the frozen flash on the Goodmoors.

Someone shouted, "Let's have a good slar"
They all joined hands for a mad carousel,
As they all fell down "hurrah hurrah.
Then a change of scene.
He was before headmaster Yates's office door.
Is it true Yates yelled you have sabotaged my car?
"Aye he said I shoved a tater up her exhaust,
it were a majestic!"

"For this filthy trick" Yates yelled, you're going to get "the stick" THE STICK".
Then in his dream, he was playing in the local team.
He scored the goal that won the Ethelston cup,
As the crowd roared.
Above the clouds his spirit soared,
They found a dead man on a bench,
With a smile on his face!

slar is a Cheshire slang for slide and **Majestic** is large heritage variety of potato

This poem is dedicated to the late Eddie Hughes - My school teacher and later in life, a close friend.

Van Love

Ladies of the county this is your chance.

I am after love.

I am seeking romance!

You might well say,

His face is very sort of lived in!

What has he got to offer?

And where has he bin?

Now it is ok. I didn't expect you to start swooning and fainting.

Because let's face it I am no oil painting,

But I Offer honesty, integrity, fidelity,

A very strong arm

I would take care of you,

and see that you did not come to any harm

But if you are looking for monogamy

Then walk on, it's not going to be,

We have been together now for 30 years

IF we had to part, it would mither me and break me, 'eart

it is all very simple really

you would just sort of buy one and get one free!

I offer practicality,

I play in a couple of bands,

But I am not a famous musician,

Or an eminent politician

But I am ever so good with me hands!

There would be no "mangage a trois"

Or anything like tha',

Our bed would just be for you and me,

As you lay sleeping there

I would love to watch the moonlight on your hair.

And gently, softly, secretly kiss your troubled brow.

I am sure we would get along just fine somehow!

I never make a fuss

And I am sure that in time love would blossom for us,

I would prove to you that I am a man!

But you would have to find room in your heart.

Not just for me but also for my lovely vintage yellow van

Panic

There were a couple of young reprobates
Called Sid Fox,
And Ronnie Bates
Who decided to blow up the cash box?
In the red phone kiosk
Down Lantern Lane, by the docks
Hey Sid! I bet there will be thirty quid,
A tenner for you and twenty for me,
What! That's not fair,
why not 50/50 fair and square?
Well I know how to mix the stuff,
YOU will just be a lackey
A look out, to trip someone up
If things get a bit rough

So they made the bomb
with the stuff the army used to use
And fitted it with a 5-minute fuse
And stuck it under the shelf
Between button A and Button B
And then retired behind a wall
"Aye Sid there will be at least a fiver for you
and the rest for me"
OH MY GOODNESS! "There is MRS Hall"
"She is going into the phone to make a call"
"I am going to stop her!"

She has been very good to me
She let me watch the footy
When we hadn,t got a Telly,
And made me a jam Butty an all!
You do and I WILL turn Queens's evidence
Tell, 'em it was you! You can't do that
I only supplied the cardboard
and the glue!

I AM NOT GOING to let the old Dearie be blown to

OH I we are all right she has stopped to light a cigarette 1

Steady there is still a minute to go!

MRS HALL MRS HALL, DON'T GO IN THERE, DON'T GO IN THERE!

I can't stop I have got to ring our Jack

Mrs Hall put her money in and pressed button A,

Hello Jack I haven't got much to say"

The dress making business is on the floor"

Then the bomb went off with a roar and

a great cloud of black smoke belched through the door,

Poor MRS Hall staggered out

covered in soot from head to floor

With her hair on end!

And shouted "YOU FILTHY BASTARDS!"

What a way to treat a friend!

Indulgance

In asking, think me not presumptuous.
We have not known each other long!
I crave an indulgence
If you would bear with me?
There are others I could find.
But it's you that I can't get out of my mind,
Join me please this autumnal night,
By a birch wood fire, burning bright
And by the fire side glow,
Look out at the barn owl, flying low.

Afterwards I would not in any measure.
Just think of my own pleasure,
but see that it was also good for you
and that you had your share of ecstasy,
Because "my dearest love,
there is nothing I would rather do,
Than lick out a Jam Jar with you!"

The Special Place

SOUTH VALLEY NURSING HOME
My birthday! 86 today, 86 today!
Will someone take me please?
To that special place by the lake,
'neath the huge aspen trees
by the big hall gates at Cherry leys.

Just leave me there, in my chair,
for an hour or two, or go away,
for half a day.
I want to be where I can listen again,
to the rustle of the leaves,
the hum of the overhead wires
and the tales that they tell.
Oh, take me please
to that special place at Cherry Leys.

And if night time should fall
and you have left me there,
Do not despair!
Do not trouble yourself at all!
I will so happy be!
Listening to the Curlews call,
at that special place by the lake,
under the huge aspen trees,
by the big hall gates at Cherry Leys.

As evening comes, shadows fall,
I want to watch the blue smoke rise,
from the chimneys at the Big Hall.
To see the rooks coming home to rest
and the little moor hens scurrying for their nest,
at that special place by the lake,
under the huge aspen trees,
by the big hall gates at Cherry Leys

My dear, dear friends from long ago.
When we played along the shore
Charley Harry, Lucy and Margo,
And lovely Debbie Moore,
Will great me there
As the sun sets, they will form,
From the mists that rise as wraiths along the shore
At that special place by the lake
Under the huge aspen trees

When you come back for me, late in the day
Do not grieve if I have been called away,
It would be remiss that I had no chance,
To say goodbye
and thank you for what you did for me!
But so happy I will be!
With my friends
An extra wraith along the shore
At that special place.
Under the huge aspen trees
By the lake at Cherry Leys.

Despair

I have got a boil, I won't tell you where!
I have got a parrot that does nothing but swear!
A cockerel that won't crow,
me car won't go,
and me girlfriend doesn't want to know!
I have got a tax bill I can't pay
Belly ache that won't go away
I am kept awake! The couple next door have orgies half the night
The hunt has passed, the road is all covered in
you have got it right!
Other things are not what they used to be
and no husband is going to be jealous of me.
The dog has cleared off to find some better company
I know that (with your platitudes) you mean well!
But you can go to hell!
It is enough to drive me to drink!
I just want to lie here and stink

Selfish Bastard

Alright, perhaps I should not have given her that stuff.

Judge me harshly, if you must!

But what good will that do?

You were not there!

You did not see the look in her eyes!

When she begged and pleaded,

alright I was weak

I gave in and let her have it.

It all started at the clinic,

When that lady doctor,

Specialist, registrar or what ever she was,

Pursed her lips to resemble an old hen's bottom,

and gave it me with both barrels,

"If you continue," she said, "putting that muck down your throat,

You have had it, you're finished, done for!"

It is up to you!

It was very hard at first!

But I overcame, didn't have any more.

And this was stuff I had already bought! Surplus, spare,

Did I give it to her so that I would not have it myself!?

In a craven weak act of self-preservation

Like I said! Judge me if you must!

But you did not see the look in her eyes

And now with all that cheese, bacon, cream, pork pies.

Cream cake, meringue, that I have given my dog,

Does she have HIGH CHOLESTEROL?

Instead of me?

Dolly

I remember her best for her gentleness, her big dark eyes, but also how warm she always was and what a huge bum she had and her scent, evocative, reminiscent of happy days.

We were the same age, kindred spirits, soul mates. Nothing needed to be said to communicate. I had loved her dearly! When I found out that they had killed her, I did my best to hit them! But I wasn't big enough, so I went frantic and tried to kick them! I was very angry. They had killed her "For money", lied to me, deceived me and treated me like a little boy. Who were these people? Gangsters or the Mafia perhaps? No! "They" were my very loving, totally devoted and supportive parents.

I was a little boy, I was eight years old, so was Dolly, she was the carthorse on the farm at Tilston in south-west Cheshire, where I was reared. It was the year 1950 and Dolly, like thousands of other folk (two as well as four legged) had been made redundant by a new machine, a tractor! When I discovered this dreadful news, it was late autumn. Having doe my best to kick or hit them and failed (they held me at arm's length) I sulked for several days. The reason I didn't get a good smacking for this was they felt badly about it too.

Two new cows could be kept on the grazing which Dolly had used, and this may well have been the difference in surviving or not on the small farm, which was my families only source of income. But try explaining this to a lonely eight-year-old lad! As far as I was concerned, Dolly was family and in my view, we should have lived or starved together!

Dolly was dark roan in colour with white "feathered" legs and a dark mane and tail, and although I thought she was huge, she was smaller than a shire horse and my Dad and Uncles referred to her as a "half legged un".

The get rid of Dolly idea started the previous spring. I came home from school one day and caught Mr. Dutton (a neighbour who did a bit of dealing) loading Dolly into a truck. "What are you doing with Dolly?!" I asked. Mum lied "She's going away to Ley". I was familiar with the Ley system, which was for cattle not horses (I didn't know that then) whereby heifers or stirks went away from the farm where they had been reared from calves, to a big field or park in a nearby village where they were looked after for the summer grazing, for a fee. These places were sometimes called Leygrounds, this took the pressure off the grazing which was needed for milking cows.

If what Mum said was true, Dolly would have returned to Finsdale farm in the autumn on the traditional "Saints day". Mum had gambled that during the summer, a long time for an eight-year old, I would forget about Dolly. I didn't! Having patiently waited all summer and into the autumn and Michaelmas Day (I think it was), having been and gone, I demanded to know when Dolly was coming back and persisted in enquiring. Mum kept putting me off by saying "Oh! You will have to ask Mr Dutton." One day, I came home from school and he was on the yard. The man I had been waiting to see for weeks – Mr Dutton!

"When's Dolly coming back?" I shouted. Mr Dutton looked very embarrassed, pathered off one foot onto the other, went a bit pink in the face and then blurted out "Er inner comin' back, 'Ers as 'er 'ed cut off!"

That's when I did the Wobbly! There has been something for Dolly to do most of the year. Basic Slag was carted out in spring and then there were the potatoes to set and I was fascinated to see the furrows made with a plough-like potato drill. The sets were placed between the furrows and then they were split with the same drill to cover the set potatoes and leave beautiful straight drills/furrows on top of them. Then there was chain harrowing and rolling on pasture as well as mowing fields. Dolly has a bit of a rest between late spring and harvest which wasn't until late June and sometime early July. The hay was carted in loose after being "made" ie turned and dried and then pickled onto the cart and then then stacked in the traditional manager which hasn't changed in century's. The lads who came to camp in our fields from Liverpool used to lead Dolly while this took place. In my mind's eye I can see them now in plimsole'd feet anxiously making sure Dolly didn't tread on them with her huge feet, but she would never have hurt them on purpose. On one occasion, my little cousin Ann, who was about three years old, fell from the front of the cart down to the back of Dolly's legs. Dolly held one of her huge feet a couple of inches above Ann's body until one of the several helpers, (the oldest man there), grabbed her petticoat and puller her clear, everyone else was rooted to the spot. I didn't think there was a problem, Dolly would have waited however long it took for Ann to be safe!

When the hay was stacked, and the fields had to be raked. Dolly would take the rake across the field at a cracking pace, and my Dad rode on top of it and at exactly the right time, pulled the lever to leave straight lines of carpet like rolls of hay. In the autumn there was much to be carted out and the fallen boughs from the trees had to be brought in and cut up for winter fuel.

Dolly's proudest job was to take someone who had died (a neighbour) on their last journey from their home up to the church yard for the funeral and burial, this happened quite often. The format was the same in most cases. When a neighbour was desperately ill, I was sent daily to enquire how they were and we would know when they had died because the muffles bell would be rung at the church. This ringing was coded and denoted gender, age and time of death of the deceased. The next of kin would come to the farm and unless it was harvest time, all work would be left, and they would be invited in to reminisce with Dad and Mum about their loved one. Due tribute would be paid to how good a hedge layer, carpenter, seamstress or cheesemaker they had been. How they would be missed! As they left, they would ask "Can you bring the mare? It's 2 o clock from the house on Saturday." Dolly would be all done up for the occasion with her name plaited, she knew that she looked good! She held her head two inches higher and was quite proud of herself and I was proud of her too!

When I had my tantrum, did I weep for Dolly or for myself and should I have wept for the end of an era?

The farming enterprise survived until July of 1999, when I retired and the last of the tractors were sold off at the farm sale. The land was sold off in chunks leaving just 12 acres remaining with the farmhouse and converted barn. The new owners kept horses, so in the end Dolly's kind survived everything else on Finsdale farm.

Last Autumn, I felt a bit nostalgic about the old place and decided to go down there and have a walk through the fields. I parked my car and had done about half my walk when I stopped to talk to a former neighbour for about half an hour during which time, it went dark. I wandered back through the field to my car, it started to flash with lightning and as it lit up the horses, my heart skipped, and there among them was a dark roan, half legged un, unmistakeably Dolly. Was this a figment of my imagination, or had she, if only for a moment, returned to the fields where she lived, worked and was loved?

Pictured above is Tilston Church. Dolly had frequent trips to the church and at least 4 generations of the authors family have been baptised here.

I express my thanks to the following people who have helped
encouraged or inspired me to write this book.

Pam Thornton who did all the drawings

Reverend Veronica Green - Vicar of Marbury, Tushingham and White Well (inspiration)

Angel and Chris Smith (who have listened to my poems)

John and Renee Gunn (officers of Whitchurch and Malpas and district Lions Club)

Teresa Carberry (District governor 2017 -2018) 105bs Lions clubs international.

Bill Brereton - for the loan of his picture TILSTON WAKES OX ROAST.

My Grandson, James Ritch for his work collating and sorting the poems.

About the Author

Dennis was born at Horton Green in the parish of Tilston near Malpas in south west Cheshire, United Kingdom, and was raised at Finsdale Farm in Tilston. Finsdale Farm was about twenty acres and was family owned but had no main water or electricity until about 1955.

The entertainment there was listening to the radio, especially Radio Luxembourg 208 meters medium wave, and also listening to a wind-up gramophone and going for walks up to the Duckington, Larkton, Bickerton Hills to pick wineberries. There were also the annual trips to the seaside, arranged by both the church and chapel for the regular attenders to the Sunday school. The annual wakes was greatly looked forward to. The wakes was a centuries-old tradition which was at one time enjoyed by many of the local villages. But Tilston Wakes outlived all the others. This was due to the efforts of many villagers, but most of all to Harry Brereton. He was chief ox roaster for many years. Harry passed on in 2002 and is fondly remembered as Mr Wakes!

Poaching game from the local estates was not entirely unheard of in Tilston!

Dennis's father died from cancer in 1965, and this prompted him to strike back. In 2005 he walked Offa's Dyke—177 miles in ten days and with the help of his friend Peter Nightingale and Whitchurh and Malpas District Lions Club. This raised £4,600, which the Lions donated to a scanner at Wythenshawe Hospital. Since then, he has lost a beloved son-in-law and sister-in-law to cancer. Due to this, Dennis has decided to donate one-third of all royalties from this book to Cancer Research UK.

Pictured above (from the left) are - Ron Blake, Arnold Williams, Lee Williams, John Hales, Tom Williams, Ronnie Rimmer, Alan Egan (chief ox roaster), Harry Brereton (veteran ox roaster) and Mayor Arthur Moore performing the traditional ox roast at the Tilston Wakes.

Printed in the United States
By Bookmasters